Rafael

The Inspirational Story of Tennis Superstar Rafael Nadal

Table Of Contents

Introduction

As the title already implies, this is a short book about [The Inspirational Story of Tennis Superstar Rafael Nadal] and how he rose from his life in Spain to becoming one of today's leading and most-respected tennis players. In his rise to superstardom, Rafael has inspired not only the youth, but fans of all ages throughout the world.

This book also portrays the struggles that Rafael has had to overcome during his early childhood years, his teen years, and up until he became who he is today. A notable source of inspiration is Rafael's service to the community and his strong connection with the fans of the sport. He continues to serve as a polarizing, entertaining superstar in a sport that certainly needs it.

Combining incredible mental fortitude, impeccable mechanics, an aggressive play style, and high tennis IQ, Rafael has shown the ability to completely dominate a match. From being a young boy who dedicated his free time to the tennis court to becoming one of the greatest tennis players of all-time, you'll learn here how this man has risen to the ranks of the best players today.

Thanks again for grabbing this book. Hopefully you can take some of the examples and lessons from Rafael's story and apply them to your own life!

Chapter 1:

Youth & Family Life

Rafael Nadal was welcomed into the world on June 3rd, 1986. He was born in Manacor, Spain to father, Sebastian, and mother, Ana Maria. Rafael was succeeded by a younger sister, Maria Isabel. Rafael was born into an athletic family and has an uncle, Miguel Angel Nadal, who had been a professional footballer for FC Barcelona, as well as for the Spanish national team.

Another uncle, Toni, became Rafael's first unofficial tennis coach. Toni had been a respectable tennis player in his own right and noticed Rafael's obvious early interest in the sport. Rafael was proactive in his training and, thanks to the encouragement of his family, he quickly developed a love for the game. By the time he was eight years old, Rafael had already won an Under-12 regional tennis tournament.

This tournament victory against other kids his age, and older, showed that Rafael had obvious potential to be a great tennis player one day. However, as with all child sports talents, Rafael would need to continue developing his game in order to stay ahead of his peers. It was after this tournament victory that Toni encouraged Rafael to switch to playing left-handed, as up until that point, he had been using two hands to hit his forehand shots.

A few years later, at the age of twelve, Rafael won the European and Spanish tennis titles for his age bracket. Along with his love for tennis, Rafael also played football competitively. However, as he progressed through his schooling years and his time became more valuable, Rafael eventually decided to leave football behind so that he could focus on tennis and his school work. The choice to focus intensely on tennis paid off soon enough, as he was invited to move to Barcelona by the Spanish Tennis Federation only two years later.

Compared to most talented child-athletes, Rafael's family made a surprising decision when the offer was presented. The family believed that Rafael did not need to be sent off to a new location to become a stronger tennis player, rather, he could continue his development at home. Even though the decision to not go meant that the family would not receive the financial incentive offered by the Spanish Tennis Federation, Sebastian decided that he would cover the necessary costs for his son's future.

Nevertheless, Rafael continued to refine his skill set and deepen his understanding of the game, eventually turning professional at the age of fifteen. He was quick to make his mark on the ITF junior circuit, playing in two events before he   turned   sixteen.

Chapter 2:

Professional Life

In his first ITF junior event, the Boy's Singles tournament held at Wimbledon, Rafael made it all the way to the semifinal round. Rafael's second and final appearance on the ITF junior circuit came when he helped lead Spain over the United States as part of the junior Davis Cup.

Not surprisingly, Rafael was awarded the Association of Tennis Professionals (ATP) "Newcomer of the Year" award for 2003.

2004 Season

The 2004 tennis season served as another stepping stone in Rafael's professional relevancy. He made it to the third round of the Australian Open before losing to Lleyton Hewitt in straight sets. At the Miami Masters, Rafael was able to defeat legend, Roger Federer, but lost to the "La Reina Bomber" Fernando Gonzalez in the fourth round.

Unfortunately, Rafael suffered a setback in the form of a stress fracture in his left ankle, causing him to miss the French Open. By the end of 2004, Rafael had jumped into fifty-first place in the world tennis ranking.

2005 Season

Rafael lost to Lleyton Hewitt once again in the 2005 Australian Open, this time in the fourth round. Rafael would go on to meet Roger Federer once again in the Miami Masters, this time losing the match after being only two points from a victory via straight sets. The match is still considered to be one of the most impressive of Federer's career.

Nevertheless, Rafael remained confident in his ability to bounce back and used these experiences as teaching moments to help his mental development along, as he was still so much younger than the majority of his competitors.

Rafael bounced back once the clay court season began, winning twenty-four straight singles matches, breaking the previous Open Era record held by Andre Agassi for the most consecutive victories by a teenager. Back in 1968, professional tennis players were finally allowed to participate in Grand Slam tournaments, which was previously for amateurs only. This started the Open Era of tennis.

Throughout his dominant run, Rafael was victorious in the Torneo Conde de Godo, the Monte Carlo Masters, and the Rome Masters. This incredible play catapulted Rafael into the top five in the world ranking. Additionally, it drew a great deal of attention to the sport, as he was being dubbed by most of the global sports media as "the future of tennis".

Such a high degree of external pressure for someone so young, especially in the entertainment/sports industry, does not always have a happy ending. However, thanks to being mentally focused and having a strong support system, Rafael used this momentum and never looked back. He entered the French Open with an outsider's chance of winning it all.

The 2005 French Open served as probably the single most important tournament of Rafael's young career, as he had a chance to really make his mark in the sport. Not only did Rafael surpass most experts' predictions on where he would finish, but he also defeated Federer in the semifinals and Mariano Puerta in the finals - an incredible feat.

Only two days after he had turned nineteen years of age, Rafael Nadal was the champion of the French Open - in his first attempt. This is also when Rafael's patented "biting of the trophy" became so popular amongst fans.

The tournament victory marked the first time a teenager had won a Grand Slam title since the legendary Pete Sampras did so fifteen years prior. Because of his impressive play over the previous few months, Rafael jumped into third place in the world ranking.

However, he was humbled once more when he lost his next match to Alexander Waske in the first round of the Gerry Weber Open. Rafael followed this performance up with a second round exit to Gilles "Mulles" Muller at the 2005 Wimbledon tournament.

Rafael bounced back from these disappointing performances, which was now becoming a trend in his career, to win his next sixteen matches, including three tournament victories. By the end of this run, he had moved into second place in the world ranking.

The remainder of Rafael's 2005 campaign included a strong performance in the Davis Cup, winning the Madrid Masters, and then an unexpected foot injury that kept him from participating in the highly anticipated Tennis Masters Cup. By the end of the roller-coaster year that was 2005, Rafael was now widely considered one of the top two players in the world, alongside Roger Federer.

Not surprisingly, he was awarded the "Most Improved Player of the Year" award by the ATP and finished the year with the highest ranking ever for a Spaniard - showing that his family was right about cultivating home-grown talent.

2006 Season

The foot injury stayed with Rafael long enough to force him to miss the 2006 Australian Open. However, he slowly regained his form by February, getting to the semifinal round at the Open 13. Rafael showed that his success on clay was not a fluke when he went on a twenty-four consecutive match win streak, including four tournaments - all on clay.

Concluding this incredible run on clay was Rafael's French Open victory against Roger Federer. In another one of the entertaining matches between the two, in what was now becoming a legendary rivalry, Rafael defeated Federer on a fourth set tiebreaker. The victory marked the first time that Federer had been defeated in a Grand Slam tournament final.

The injury bug bit Rafael again and he was forced to take some time off because of a shoulder injury suffered at the Queen's Club. Because he was unable to complete the match against Hewitt, Rafael's twenty-six match winning streak came to an end. After a successful rehabilitation, Rafael defeated Andre Agassi in what would become Agassi's last match at Wimbledon.

Upon making it to the final round, Rafael met Federer, who had been victorious at Wimbledon in each of the previous three years. Federer continued his brilliance at Wimbledon by beating Rafael, despite a valiant effort by the Spaniard. Upon season's end, Rafael became the first player since Andre Agassi to finish as the number two ranked player for consecutive years.

2007 Season

Rafael started the next season by taking part in six straight hard-court tournaments. After a mixture of successes and disappointments, Rafael found his groove again once he returned to clay. He went on to win the Monte Carlo Masters, the Open Sabadell, and the Rome Masters. He totaled eighty-one straight victories on clay, setting the Open Era record for the most consecutive victories on a single surface. As expected, Rafael then took the French Open for the third straight year.

After a loss in the quarterfinals of the Artois Championships at the Queen's Club, Rafael entered Wimbledon in hopes to win his first championship there. After third and fourth round matches that each went five sets, Rafael met Federer in the final round once again. The final match went five sets with Federer able to pull through at the end.

Rafael's last title victory of the year came in July, when he was victorious at the Mercedes Cup in Stuttgart. He went deep into the Rogers Cup and the US Open but was unable to advance past the semifinal round. As the year came to an end, Rafael took part in the Tennis Masters Cup, winning two out of his three round robin matches. However, he ultimately lost to Federer.

The second half of the 2007 season certainly did not meet Rafael's expectations but it was largely due to dealing with a knee injury that he incurred in the Wimbledon finals match.

2008 Season

Rafael was looking to push his legacy to the next level in 2008, as he started the year with his deepest run at the Australian Open yet, making it to the semifinal round. The spring clay-court season was prosperous for Rafael, as he earned four titles, defeating Federer in three of them.

Rafael's dominance at the French Open continued, where he took the Grand Slam title without losing a single set. He met Federer in the final round once again, this time defeating him in lopsided fashion - giving Federer a bagel.

In the next stage of the rapidly developing Nadal-Federer rivalry, the two met in the Wimbledon finals for the third straight year. The match was even more highly anticipated than usual because Rafael entered the showdown on a twenty-three match winning streak while Federer had not lost a single set leading up to the final round.

With much to prove on the court and with the whole sports world watching, Rafael was able to finally break through on Wimbledon grass. The match was the lengthiest in the history of the tournament, mainly due to rain delays. However, it was very closely contested and there never appeared to be a clear-cut favorite in the match. Rafael took the fifth set by a score of 9-7 after the sun had already disappeared from sight.

Afterwards, the match was praised by many as the greatest Wimbledon final of all-time, some experts even claiming that it was the single greatest match in the history of the sport.

This victory at Wimbledon not only served as a mental breakthrough for Rafael, who had been on the cusp of Wimbledon victory for the past three years, but it also made him only the third man in the Open Era to win the French and Wimbledon in the same year.

The momentum continued to roll, as Rafael took home the Rogers Cup title and reached the semifinal round of the Western & Southern Masters at Cincinnati. After Rafael clinched the US Open Series, combined with Federer struggling to advance in consecutive tournaments, Rafael was now the number one ranked player in the world.

As a very patriotic man, one of Rafael's greatest honors and accomplishments came when he was able to win the gold medal for Spain at the 2008 Beijing Olympics. He followed up the Olympics with a run into the semifinal round of the US Open, in which he entered as the number one seeded player. Rafael won for his country once again by helping Spain defeat the United States in the Davis Cup.

After being forced to retire in the quarterfinal round of the BNP Paribas Masters because of a knee injury, Rafael withdrew from the Tennis Masters Cup due to a diagnosis of tendinitis. Nevertheless, Rafael finished the year as the top ranked player in the world after Federer had held that title for the previous four and a half years.

2009 Season

With the Australian Open title having been so elusive for Rafael, he entered the 2009 tournament on a mission to finally get it. After getting through his first five matches without dropping a single set, Rafael met Fernando Verdasco in a semifinals match that lasted over five hours - the second longest match in the history of the Australian Open. Upon advancing to the final round, Rafael met Federer once more, though it was only the first time they had met on a hard-court Grand Slam final.

Rafael emerged victorious in five sets of spectacular play, taking home his first Grand Slam title on a hard-court, making him the only Spaniard to ever win the Australian Open. Additionally, it showed Rafael's diversity as a player that could seriously compete at the highest level on any court surface. The tournament victory also made Rafael the first player to simultaneously hold three different Grand Slam titles from three different surfaces.

Rafael suffered another injury to his knee at the ABN World Tennis Tournament in Rotterdam, forcing him to withdraw from the Barclays Tennis Championships held the following week. After recovering from his tendon injury. Rafael helped Spain defeat Serbia in the Davis Cup World Group before winning the Monte Carlo Masters for the fifth consecutive year.

Soon after, Rafael won the Rome Masters once again, his fourth title victory there. Just as it seemed that Rafael could never lose on clay, he suffered a surprising loss in the fourth round of the French Open to the hands of Robin Soderling.

After the loss at Roland Garros, Rafael decided to withdraw from the AEGON Championships to recover from his lingering tendonitis pain. He did not participate in Wimbledon either, hoping to give himself ample recovery time.

After Federer won the Wimbledon title in mid-2009, Rafael moved back to the number two spot in the world ranking. In December, Rafael spearheaded Spain's victory at the Davis Cup,

giving him fourteen consecutive singles victories
at the event.

2010 Season

Rafael won the Capitala World Tennis Championship to start off his 2010 season, defeating Soderling in the final round via straight sets. However, after a promising start at the Australian Open, Rafael was told by doctors that he needed to take a month off for rest and rehabilitation before continuing on court.

Rafael returned to familiar territory when he reached the final round of the Monte Carlo Masters. He won the final match in straight sets against Fernando Verdasco. The impressive tournament performance saw Rafael only drop fourteen total games throughout all five of the matches. The tournament victory also made Rafael the first player in the Open Era to win the same tournament in six consecutive years.

After taking the Madrid Open, Rafael became the first player in the history of the sport to win all three of the clay-court Masters in the same year. Additionally, he became the only player to ever win three straight Masters events.

With the sports world in anticipation of a Nadal-Federer final round at the French Open, a surprising turn of events saw Federer go down to Soderling in the quarterfinals. Rafael eventually went on to win the tournament by defeating Soderling in the final round. Rafael put on another incredible show throughout the French Open, getting through the tournament without dropping a single set.

The combination of an early exit by Federer, along with the dominant performance by Rafael, moved him back into the number one spot in the world ranking.

In June, Rafael made it to the quarterfinal round of the AEGON Championships before being defeated by Feliciano Lopez. At Wimbledon, Rafael defeated Kei Nishikori, Robin Haase, Philipp Petzschner, Paul-Henri Mathieu, Robin Soderling, and Andy Murray en route to a finals match-up against Tomas Berdych. In what was

Rafael's fourth straight Wimbledon finals appearance, he defeated Berdych in straight sets.

Rafael candidly thanked the crowd after winning the event, even stating that taking Wimbledon was "more than a dream" for him. The tournament victory served as the eighth career major title for Rafael - though he had only just turned twenty-four. Having now won the Italian Open, French Open, and Wimbledon all in 2010, Rafael had won the prestigious "Old World Triple". The feat was last accomplished by Bjorn Borg thirty-two years prior.

Rafael made it to the semifinal round of the Rogers Cup before losing to rising star, Andy Murray. Murray's victory was the second over Rafael during 2010. Soon after, Rafael entered the US Open as the top seeded player, the second time in his last three appearances. With the US Open being the last major title for him to win, fans were glued to their television in hopes to see the Spaniard win it all.

Rafael did not disappoint, as he defeated Gabashvili, Istomin, Simon, Lopez, Verdasco, and Youzhny all without dropping a single set. This beautiful performance set the stage for a Nadal-Djokovic final in which Rafael was victorious.

The 2010 US Open victory put Rafael in the record books for many different accomplishments, including becoming the second youngest to ever reach the final round of all four majors, as well as the second male to complete a Career Golden Slam, after Agassi.

Additionally, Rafael became the only man to ever win majors on hard court, grass court, and clay court surfaces in a single year. He was also the first male to win the French, Wimbledon, and US Open in a single year since Rod Laver did so over forty years prior.

Rafael followed the US Open with a title victory at the Japan Open Tennis Championships before announcing in early November that he was pulling out of the Paris Masters because of tendinitis in his left shoulder. After all was said and done, Rafael's 2010 season is considered to be one of the best years by a male tennis player that we have ever seen. Not only was Rafael dominant in his Grand Slam title victories, but he also went deep into the tournaments that he did not win.

For his outstanding year, Rafael was awarded the Stefan Edberg Sportsmanship Award in late November and his season's resume featured three Grand Slam titles, three Masters 1000 tournaments and the year's completion as the number one ranked player in the world. As the 2010 year concluded, it became hard to find detractors saying that Rafael could not dominate on surfaces other than clay and he was now in the discussion for the top ten players of all time, despite his young age.

2011 Season

Rafael started the 2011 season with a title victory at the Mubadala World Tennis Championship, defeating Federer in the final round. He then fell in the semifinal round of the Qatar Open to Nikolay Davydenko, having dealt with a fever throughout the tournament. However, he and fellow Spaniard, Lopez, were able to win the tournament's doubles title.

In an attempt to win four straight major tournaments, Rafael fell to David Ferrer in the quarterfinal round of the Australian Open after suffering an untimely hamstring injury. Good news soon followed, when in early February, Rafael was awarded the distinguished honor of "Laureus World Sportsman of the Year" for the first time in his career. He was given the award over Lionel Messi, Kobe Bryant, Manny Pacquiao, and Andres Iniesta.

Soon after, Rafael helped Spain win the 2011 Davis Cup World Group after a victory against Olivier Rochus in the second dead rubber match. In the BNP Paribas Open, Rafael met Juan Martin del Potro in the semifinal round, who had defeated him in their previous three meetings. Rafael started strong and never looked back, taking the victory via straight sets. After reaching the final round, Rafael was defeated by Djokovic.

Only two weeks later, Rafael met Djokovic in the final round once again - this time as part of the 2011 Ericsson Open. After a very hard-fought battle in the first three sets, Djokovic emerged on top by winning a tiebreak in the third set. Despite the two straight losses to Djokovic, it marked the first time in Rafael's career that he had reached the final round of the Indian Wells and Miami in a single year.

Rafael bounced back quickly, winning the Monte Carlo Masters tournament while only dropping a single set on his path. With this tournament victory, Rafael became the only man in the history of the Open Era to win the same event seven consecutive times at the ATP level. A week later, Rafael won his sixth title at the Barcelona

Open, defeating Ferrer in the final round via straight sets. By doing so, Rafael added to his long list of accomplishments by becoming the only male in the history of the sport to win two tournaments six times each.

Rafael fell to Djokovic once more upon reaching the final round of the Madrid Open, after defeating Baghdatis, del Potro, Llodra, and Federer. A surprising result occurred when Djokovic defeated Rafael in the Rome Masters final - marking the first time that Rafael had lost on clay to the same player in a single year. The victory also marked the rise to dominance for Novak Djokovic, as he was slowly but surely making a case for the top overall spot in the world ranking.

However, as we now know about Rafael, he was not content to let a personal slump last for long, and he quickly regained focus entering the French Open. He was able to put on some very impressive performances en route to a sixth French Open title after defeating Federer in the final round.

At Wimbledon, Rafael defeated Murray in the semifinal round, setting up a final round match with Djokovic. After a very competitive match, Djokovic pulled away in the fourth set and it marked Rafael's first loss at Wimbledon since the five set match to Federer in the 2007 final.

Not surprising to many, the victory pushed Djokovic into first place in the world ranking for the first time ever. The Serb had finally broken the run of dominance by Nadal and Federer. Combined, Rafael and Roger had held the number one position every single week since February of 2004.

The nagging foot injury re-appeared in Wimbledon and Rafael decided to take about a month off from competition. However, after beating David Nalbandian in the fourth round at the US Open, Rafael collapsed during the post-match press conference due to extreme cramps. He was able to play in the final against Djokovic but there were certainly some after-effects from the cramping. However, he was able to defeat Federer in straight sets at the Mubadala World Tennis Championship upon year's end.

2012 Season

Though he felt less than satisfied in his personal tennis endeavors for the year, 2011 marked the fourth time that Rafael had helped the Spanish team win the Davis Cup, along with 2004, 2008, and 2009. In early 2012, Rafael defeated Alex Kuznetsov, Tommy Haas, Lopez, Berdych, and Federer before meeting Djokovic in the 2012 Australian Open final.

This impressive run marked a consecutive finals appearance in all four majors for Rafael. The final round match between Rafael and Djokovic was one for the ages, going seven minutes shy of a six hour match. It was also the longest ever match at a Grand Slam title, Djokovic prevailed in the end.

After a semifinal run at Indian Wells, followed by a semifinal appearance at Miami, Rafael chose to withdraw because of knee pain. He took some time off to recover before starting the clay court season. At the Monte Carlo Masters, Rafael met Djokovic in the final round once again, this time defeating the Serb to win the event for the eighth straight time. Additionally, Rafael's victory over Djokovic snapped a seven match losing streak against him.

Rafael continued to show why he was the master of the clay court, defeating David Ferrer in a grueling battle at the Barcelona Open. By winning Barcelona, Rafael had won seven titles in eight years. He lost at the Madrid Open to Fernando Verdasco, whom he had previously held a 13-0 record against. After the tournament, Rafael, Djokovic, and many other players voiced their criticism of the change from red to blue colored clay.

Rafael continued building his impressive resume on clay as he defeated Djokovic in the finals of the Internazionali BNL d'Italia in Rome - his sixth title at the event. The French Open was a spark for Rafael. He only dropped a total of thirty games against his first five opponents and did not lose a single set. Rafael followed this up with another near perfect match against David Ferrer in the semifinal round. Upon meeting Djokovic in the final round of the French, it marked the first time in history that the same two players met in four consecutive Grand Slam tournament finals.

After a decisive victory by Rafael in the first two sets, Djokovic responded with an impressive third set. Soon after, rain had started to pick up and the fourth set was suspended until the following day. Rafael won the match the next day after Djokovic double faulted on match point. The victory marked the seventh title at Roland Garros for Rafael - the most ever by a male player. By tournament's end, Rafael had only lost one set, which came in the final round. In total, Rafael only lost three sets in the entirety of his 2012 clay court season.

Rafael lost at Wimbledon in the second round before he made the decision to withdraw from the 2012 Olympics because of tendinitis in his knee. As the recovery took longer than expected, Rafael decided to stay out of the Rogers Cup, Cincinnati Masters, and US Open as well.

Because he was forced to take such an extended time away from the court, Rafael was moved into fourth place in the world ranking, as Andy

Murray was promoted to number three.

2013 Season

As you can expect by now, with Rafael going through a downward slide to end 2012, it would only be normal for him to bounce back in glorious fashion. However, just as he was ready to start the 2013 season with a vengeance, he suffered a stomach virus two weeks before the Australian Open. Unfortunately, his withdrawal meant that he was now out of the top four in the ATP ranking for the first time since 2005.

Rafael made his first tournament return count, as he won the 2013 Brasil Open, despite dealing with a sub-par clay surface - a common complaint amongst players in attendance. Rafael's next title match was at the 2013 Abierto Mexicano Telcel, in which he defeated fellow Spaniard, David Ferrer. The performance featured only two lost games by Rafael.

Upon returning to the United States, Rafael entered the Indian Wells Masters as the fifth seeded player. On his path to the final round, he defeated Federer and Berdych while only losing one total set. The final match featured a comeback by Rafael, coming back from one set down to defeat del Potro in dramatic fashion.

After withdrawing from Miami and losing in the final of the Monte Carlo Masters, Rafael won the Barcelona Open in straight sets. The victory at Barcelona made Rafael the first male to win two separate tournaments at least eight times. Additionally, the tournament victory marked the fourth title of the season and sixth straight final for Rafael.

After being only two points from defeat in the quarterfinal against Ferrer in the 2013 Madrid Open, Rafael dominated the rest of the way. The tournament victory meant that he had now won twenty-three ATP Masters 1000 tournaments. Soon after, Rafael took the 2013 Rome Masters as well, defeating Federer in the final round. Upon reaching the near halfway point in the year, Rafael was now back into fourth place in the world ranking.

Rafael's momentum continued as he won the French Open for the eighth time, this time defeating Djokovic in the semifinal and Ferrer in the final. Djokovic and Rafael had another epic battle at the French, one in which Nadal came back from a break down in the last set to take the victory. The match lasted over four and a half hours and is considered to be one of the greatest clay-court matches ever.

After a disappointing first round loss to Steve Darcis at Wimbledon, Rafael bounced back to win the Rogers Cup over Milos Raonic in the final round via straight sets. Rafael found himself matched up against Djokovic once more in the 2013 US Open final, this time resulting in a victory for Rafael in four sets. The victory at the US Open brought Rafael's Grand Slam title count to thirteen.

Now that Rafael had proven he was back in dominant shape, he slowly moved up the rankings until he secured the number one overall spot by winning the ATP World Tour Finals in November.

2014 Season

Rafael's 2014 season was quite a productive one, with a record of 48 wins against only 11 losses. Those wins translated to four titles and a number 3 world ranking.

He was off to a good start with a win in the Qatar ExxonMobil Open. "Rafa", then World Number 1 and the tournament's first seed, defeated Gael Monfils in three sets - 6-1, 6-7, 6-2 - to earn the coveted Falcon Trophy. This was his first Qatar Open Singles win after five previous tries, though he did succeed in the Doubles events thrice.

In the Australian Open held in January, Rafael lost his chance to regain the title he last won in 2009. Before the championship match, he had to go through Bulgarian Grigor Dimitrov, Kei Nishikori, and Roger Federer. In the last match of the tournament, Rafael lost in four sets against a determined Stanislas Wawrinka - who won his first Grand Slam singles title.

Stan the Man or "Stanimal", who hails from Switzerland, won 6-3, 6-2, 3-6, 6-3. Rafael suffered a back injury during the second set and the game had to be stopped for a while. The hurting Rafael returned to the game and was able to win the third set before Stan put a damper on his comeback. This marked the second time Rafael finished as runner-up in the tournament.

Rafael racked up another title in February, this time at the inaugural Rio Open tournament. The new tennis event falls under the ATP World Tour 500 series category and was held at the Jockey Club Brasileiro. The top two seeds were the Number 1 Nadal and compatriot David Ferrer, ranked third in the world. Other top-ranked participants were No. 13 Nico Almagro of Spain, No. 16 Italian Fabio "Fogna" Fognini, and 18th ranked Spaniard Tomy Robredo.

Rafael beat fellow Spaniards Daniel Gimeno-Traver and Albert Montanes in the first two rounds before beating Portuguese Joao Sousa in the quarterfinals. He faced off with another Spanish player in Pablo Andujar in the semis before advancing to the title match. Rafael beat Alexandr "The Dog" Dolgopolov, 6-3, 7-6. The win was his 62nd title on the tour level.

In March, Rafael participated in the Indian Wells Masters where he received a bye into the second round. He disposed of Radek Stepanek in three sets, setting up a rematch with Dolgopolov. This time, however, The Dog exacted revenge on the King of Clay, 6-3, 3-6, 7-6. Dolgopolov advanced to the semifinals but met a tougher Roger Federer. Djokovic ended up as the winner of the tournament after defeating Federer in the finals.

Rafael then flew to Florida to play in the Miami Masters. He rolled easily through the early rounds with convincing wins over three other players. In those three matches, he only lost nine games. He faced Milos Raonic in the quarters and emerged victorious. Later on, he and Djokovic received walkovers and allowed both tennis greats to rekindle their rivalry. Unfortunately for Rafael, their 40th head-to-head ended with "The Djoker" prevailing in two sets.

Rafael would later fail to win the title in the next two tournaments he joined. At the Monte Carlo Masters, he breezed through the early rounds and even won his 300th clay court victory at the expense of Andreas Seppi. He hit the proverbial wall in the quarterfinals, as David Ferrer got the better of him. At the Barcelona Open, Rafael again fell during the quarterfinals, this time to Nicolas Almagro.

Rafael's fortunes would change at the Madrid Open as he won the event against Kei Nishikori. The win gave him the fourth Madrid Open title of his career. At the Italian Open, Djokovic would again prove to be the thorn in Nadal's side. The loss prevented Rafael from claiming his eighth Italian Open title in nine finals appearances. The King of Clay finished the spring clay court season with a win over Djokovic at the French Open. It was his ninth title at the event.

Rafael suffered a wrist injury while practicing and had to pull out of the Canadian Open, Cincinnati Masters, and US Open. He recovered in time for the China Open where he won the first two rounds but was defeated by Martin Klizan during the quarterfinals. He'd have almost the same results at the Shanghai Masters. Rafael lost in his first match against Feliciano Lopez.

His poor performance can be attributed to appendicitis. Rafa was suffering from the ailment but didn't want to go under the knife until the season was finished. After a defeat at the hands of teenager Borna Coric at the Swiss Indoors, Rafael decided to withdraw from the Paris Masters and ATP World Tour Finals.

2015 Season

The following season saw Rafael falling to fifth place in the world ranking. He finished with a win-loss record of 61-20. His first tournament ended in disaster as Rafael lost in the first round of the Qatar Masters against Michael Berrer, ranked 127th at the time. Nadal and Juan Monaco did manage to grab the Doubles title though.

He made it to the quarterfinals of the Australian Open after going through Mikhail Youzhny, Tim Smyczek, Dudi Sela, and Kevin Anderson. However, Tomas Berdych notched his first win after 17 losses to Nadal.

Rafael suffered a semifinal loss at the Rio Open after plowing through Thomaz Bellucci, Pablo Carreno Busta, and Pablo Cuevas in consecutive rounds. His loss to Fabio Fognini was the first in their head-to-head match-up. Rafael vastly upped his game at the Argentina Open as he outclassed everyone, including finalist Jun

Monaco. He won the Argentina Open crown without losing a single set. This was his 46th title on a clay court.

Rafael won against some tough competitors in his early matches of the Monte-Carlo Masters, but faced off with an even tougher one in world number 1 Novak Djokovic during the semifinals. Rafael avenged his 2013 Barcelona Open loss to Nicolas Almagro with an impressive straight set win in the second round. But as fate would have it, Rafael would lose in straight sets to Fabio Fognini in the third round.

Rafael was able to get back to his winning ways by defeating Denmark's Mikael Torpegaard in the singles event of the Davis Cup. He reached the final of the China Open after defeating Wu Di, Vasek Pospisil, Jack Sock, and Fabio Fognini. However, he lost to Djokovic in the final match.

Rafael reached the semifinal of the Shanghai Rolex Masters but was defeated by Jo-Wilfried Tsonga in three sets. He made it to the finals of the Swiss Indoors ATP 500 as well, which he eventually lost to Roger Federer.

2016 Season

The 8th Mubadala World Tennis Championship was held from December 31st, 2015 to January 2nd, 2016. Those three days saw six of the top 14 ranked tennis players from all over the world duke it out in the Abu Dhabi International Tennis Complex. When the smoke cleared, Rafael was left standing tall after beating Canadian Milos Raonic, the sixth seed in the tournament, 7-6, 6-3. The second-seeded Rafael made up for his losses in the previous two years' edition. He also made $250,000 out of the tournament.

He followed that great start of the year with a loss, however. Two days after claiming the Mubadala title, Rafael joined seven other top ranked tennis vets, which included number one ranked Novak Djokovic in the 24th Qatar ExxonMobil Open at the Khalifa International and Squash Complex. At the end of the six-day tournament, Djokovic emerged victorious in the singles event, edging out Nadal, 6-1, 6-2.

Out of the 47 times Nadal and Djokovic have faced each other on the tennis court, the latter came out with a victory 24 times. All in all, Rafael is just one win shy of equaling his rival. This is arguably one of the greatest rivalries in the history of tennis.

In January, Rafael lost in the first round of the Australian Open to Fernando Verdasco - marking the first time he did not make it out of the first round of a Grand Slam tournament. However, as we know by now, Rafael bounced back quickly. He was able to emerge victorious at the Monte Carlo Rolex Masters Men's singles tournament.

The win marked his ninth Monte Carlo Masters crown. Additionally, it was his 48th clay court title, putting him just behind the Argentinian legend Guillermo Vilas, who finished with 49 clay court titles to his name.

Rafael took advantage of his momentum by winning another title while playing in his own country this time. The Barcelona Open was held on the clay courts of Real Club de Tenis

Barcelona and is part of the ATP World Tour 500 series. Rafael took down Fabio Fognini in the quarterfinals and proceeded to dismantle Philipp Kohlschreiber in the semifinal round, on his way to the title match against defending champion Kei Nishikori.

Rafael's two set victory over the two-time winner was the ninth Barcelona Open title for the Spaniard. It was also nine out of the 24 total wins by a Spaniard in the said tournament since it started in 1953. Rafael also tied Vilas at 49 clay court tournament wins in the Open Era.

At this point, Rafael holds the distinction of having the most titles in three different Singles tournaments in the Open Era. He now has nine titles each in the Monte Carlo, Barcelona, and Roland Garros events.

Chapter 3:

Personal Adult Life

Rafael is not only one of the greatest tennis players to ever play the sport but he is a very unique and interesting person off the court as well.

Because he grew up with an uncle who played professional football, Rafael has always had an interest in the sport. He is an avid fan of the football club, Real Madrid, as well as RCD Mallorca. He has even become a shareholder in his hometown team and even though he declined the offer, he has been offered executive positions within the organization.

In addition to his local and club team support, Rafael is also a huge supporter of the Spanish national team. He has become such an enthusiast that he was one of only six people not affiliated with the team or national federation, that was allowed to enter the team's locker room after they won the 2010 FIFA World Cup. Rafael also loves to play golf and poker whenever he gets the chance.

Many fans of Rafael, especially younger ones, have stated that he reminds them of a super-hero. Whether it be his unique style, his long hair, or his ripped shoulders and arms, it is easy to see why they perceive him as such. Maybe the roots for this is that Rafael grew up as a huge fan of Dragon Ball, specifically Goku. He used to run home from school in order to watch each day's episode of the anime.

In 2011, Rafael and John Carlin published his autobiography, entitled *Rafa*. If you are a big fan of Rafael, the autobiography is a great place to learn about many of his life events through his own perspective.

As an interesting aside, the Observatorio Astronomic de Mallorca discovered a main belt asteroid in 2003 and decided to name it 128036 Rafaelnadal, as a tribute to their hometown star.

Chapter 4:

Philanthropic/Charitable Acts

An admirable part of Rafael's personality is that he has made sure to use his fame and worldwide platform to give back to those who are less fortunate. In 2007, Rafael created the Fundacion Rafa Nadal and he publicly presented it in February of 2008.

The foundation's focus is to provide social work and development in the form of giving back to the youth. It provides opportunities for children to succeed when they might not otherwise be given a fair chance.

Rafael's mother, Ana Maria, runs the charitable organization and his father is the vice-chairman. His other family members also help with the operations of the organization and have helped it grow into a very impactful force. Rafael has drawn inspiration to help those living in poverty in India as well as to help build the communities of the Balearic Islands of Spain.

In addition to having his own foundation, Rafael has also supported City Harvest, Small Steps Project, Elton John AIDS Foundation, and a host of other charitable groups. He can often be seen participating at the charity events hosted by other philanthropists and celebrities, including fellow tennis players and even football players.

He joins in whenever he can, helping to add more engagement from the community, and even donates his own money to some of these causes. One such event included the two-match exhibition hosted by Roger Federer in 2010, as part of the Roger Federer Foundation.

In 2013, Rafael took part in a charity poker tournament against legendary Brazilian footballer, Ronaldo, along with poker great Daniel Negreanu, retired football player Andriy Shevchenko, skier Alberto Tomba, and Fatima

Morera de Melo of field hockey fame. Proving he has talents other than smashing a ball with a racket, Rafael won the European Poker Tour (EPT) Charity Challenge. He donated a portion of the pot money to The Good Hand Project.

Rafa has also lent his talents to the Annual Necker Cup Tennis Pro-Am. In its three years of existence, the event has garnered around $2.5 million, which has been used in various charitable causes.

In early 2015, Rafael faced off with Fernando Verdasco in "Rafa's Summer Set", an exhibition match that aims to gather funds for charity. The event, held in Melbourne, also featured Australian Mark Philippoussis and Omar Jasika, winner of junior singles.

Rafael also played in another charity event in 2015 - this time for John McEnroe Tennis Academy, which focuses on helping young tennis players who are having a difficult time financially.

Rafael will participate in the 17th Annual Taste of Tennis known as the World's Premier Food and Tennis Experience. The event combines the glitz and glamour of professional tennis and the culinary arts. Top celebrity chefs and tennis pros participate in this yearly event to give their support to its cause. The Taste of Tennis event, which started in 2000, benefits various charitable projects.

This year, the proceeds will go to Wellness In The Schools (WITS), a non-profit organization that promotes good health among public school children through healthier eating and exercise. One of the advocacies of WITS is to have healthier options in school cafeterias and to educate children about the importance of proper nutrition and fitness.

Rafael has also sanctioned the creation of a tennis academy that caters to underprivileged children in Anantapur City. In 2010, Rafa went on a trip to India to see for himself how his tennis academy was progressing. That was how much he invested of himself in his foundation and his efforts to reach out to the world.

Rafael has stated that he looks forward to getting more physically involved in his philanthropic endeavors upon retirement from the sport, when he will have much more free time to give. Nonetheless, he has already made such a huge impact in the world for a man who is still so young in life.

Chapter 5:

Legacy, Potential & Inspiration

As a player profile, Rafael is known for his aggressive, powerful style of play. He likes to play behind the baseline while using heavy topspin on his groundstrokes. He is obviously a physical specimen to the eye, one that moves well and is usually athletically superior to his opponents.

One of his advantages is his ability to cover the court and use his footwork to run down well-placed shots. Because of this, he is considered to be one of the best counter hitters and defenders that the sport has seen in quite a few years.

Often times, it seems as if Rafael will not be able to make a play on the ball or is in a completely defensive position, yet somehow finds a way to respond with an off-balance winning shot. Rafael uses the drop shot well and mixes it in with his heavy topspin shots to keep his opponents always guessing. He also uses an unorthodox full western grip on his forehand that allows him to use much more topspin than his opponents are accustomed to - a great advantage for him.

The great debate regarding Rafael's powerful, forceful style of play, especially when compared to the more surgical, less vicious style of play of Federer, is something that has always surrounded Rafael's career. Because he is such a polarizing force, "experts" love to discuss how Rafael should play less aggressive or not rely as much on his physical skills.

However, what many of these detractors do not bring up is the fact that Rafael's style of play has been as effective as any other style of play. Additionally, Rafael has drawn a great deal of casual fans to the sport, those who might not be as well-versed in the technical skills of tennis but rather want to see the physical feats that players are capable of.

While he certainly puts more torque on his knees, evident by his recurring knee pain and tendinitis, when Rafael is playing at his best he is considered to be one of the best players that the game has ever seen.

Longevity is important in the sport of tennis, but being explosive and powerful can provide benefits as well - and is extremely hard to defend against. It is not the physical dominance that makes Rafael an elite player, it is the combination of his physical dominance along with his mental understanding and technical abilities that keep him at the top.

Nonetheless, at the end of the day, as tennis fans, we are certainly blessed to be watching the tennis of this era. Nadal, Federer, Djokovic, Murray, Serena Williams, and others are making this the most exciting time to be a tennis fan and are providing us with so many different skills and styles that we can enjoy.

Conclusion

Hopefully this book was able to help you gain inspiration from the life of Rafael Nadal, one of the best tennis players in the world.

Rafael serves as a great representative for Spain, Europe, and the sport of tennis. His respectful demeanor and understanding of the legends before him makes it very hard for someone to dislike him. Additionally, he is able to keep fans glued to the television because they know that any time he plays in a competition, there is a possibility that he will make history.

Rafael has inspired so many people because he is the star who never fails to connect with fans and give back to the less fortunate. Noted for his ability to dominate the competition on any day, he is a joy to watch on the court. Last but not least, he's remarkable for remaining simple and firm with his principles in spite of his immense popularity.

Hopefully you've learned some great things about Rafael in this book and are able to apply some of the lessons that you've learned to your own life! Good luck in your journey!

Printed by Amazon Italia Logistica S.r.l.
Torrazza Piemonte (TO), Italy

16423341R00041